Zen paths to Change

Zen paths to Change

Journey Editions
Boston • Tokyo • Singapore

Introduction

It is through change that we learn and grow as individuals. Zen teaches us to seek out our true selves—our own talents and creativity—rather than conforming to what is expected or demanded of us. Follow your intuition, be true to yourself, and you will make the right choices in life. For most of us, this is a hard path to tread. We find ourselves thrust into a world where individual success is dictated by promotion, financial success, and social standing. The Zen approach to change is to listen to the inner voice, find the courage to be yourself, and make the necessary changes that will help you follow your own path. In essence to find your *dharma* (or calling), and listen to your heart's teaching.

Drawing on themes of responsibility, self-confidence, discipline, and perseverance, the quotations and images in this book reveal how we can take a Zen approach to change. The teachings are drawn from great spiritual works, such as the *Tao te Ching*, *The Blue Cliff Record*, and the *Bible*, together with sayings of Zen Masters and students, and the ideas of Western thinkers and writers. The paths do not promote an aggressive or selfish course of action but rather a quiet awakening and a summoning of inner bravery and passion that will lead to greater personal fulfillment.

The only way to make sense out of change
is to **plunge** with it,
move with it,
and **join the dance**.

Alan Watts

Teachers open the door,

but you must **enter** by yourself.

Chinese proverb

Looking
forward only,
Unknowing how
to turn **back**.

Sayings of the Masters

Gingerly,
carefully
look in the abyss;

Walk

on thin ice.

Sayings of the Masters

One sees great things from the valley, only small things from the peak.

G. K. Chesterton

A man with outward courage

dares to die

A man with inward courage
dares to live.

Lao Tzu

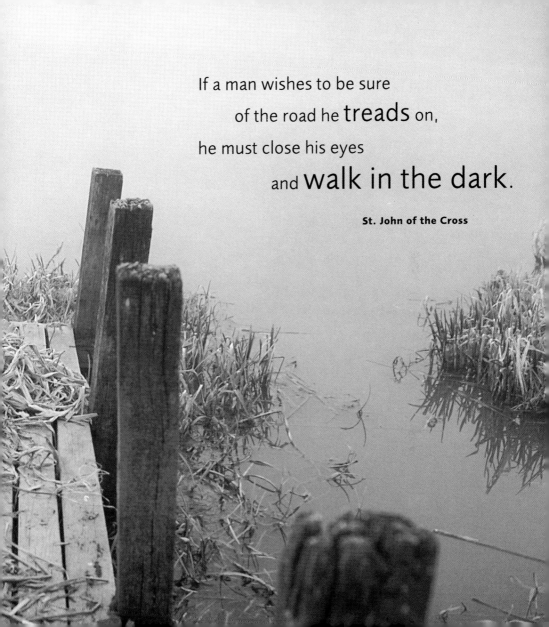

If a man wishes to be sure
of the road he **treads** on,
he must close his eyes
and **walk in the dark.**

St. John of the Cross

There is no security in life,
only opportunity.

Mark Twain

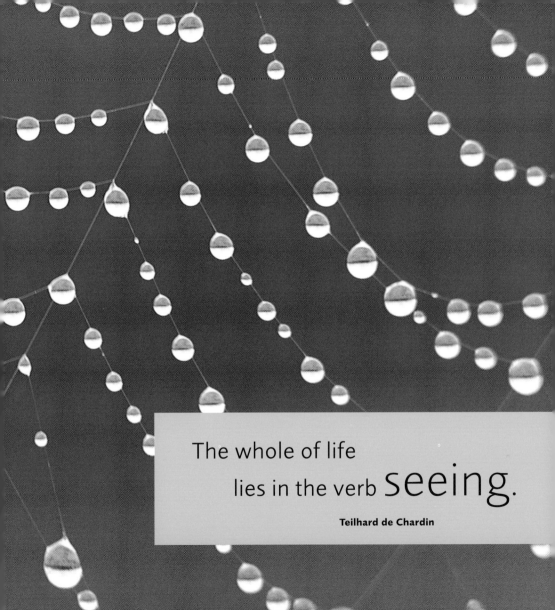

The whole of life
lies in the verb seeing.

Teilhard de Chardin

Go—not knowing where.

Bring—not knowing what.

The path is long,

the way unknown.

Russian fairy tale

Never compose anything
unless the **not composing** of it
becomes a positive nuisance to you.

Gustav Holst

The Ultimate Path is without difficulty;
Just avoid picking and choosing.

The Blue Cliff Record

If our nature is permitted to guide our life,

we grow **healthy, fruitful** and **happy**.

Abraham Maslow

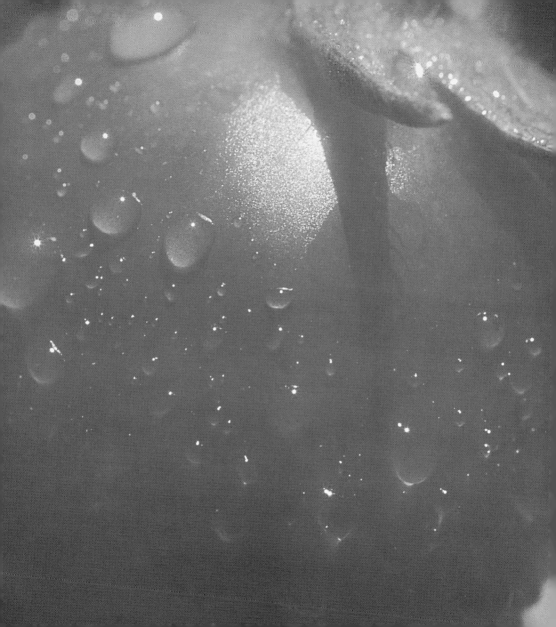

The most terrifying thing is to
accept oneself completely.

Carl Jung

Go **confidently** in the direction

of your dreams.

Act as though it were

impossible to fail.

Dorthea Brandt

The future belongs to
those who believe in
the **beauty** of their dreams.

Eleanor Roosevelt

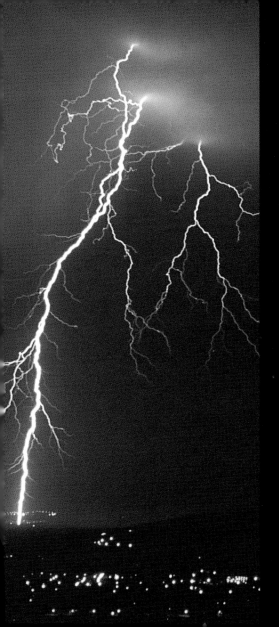

Whatever you do
or dream you can do
—**begin it**.
Boldness has
genius and **power**
and **magic** in it.

Goethe

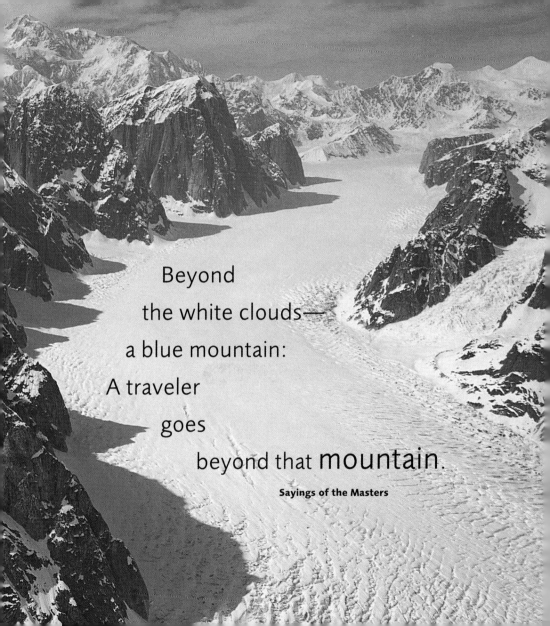

Beyond
the white clouds—
a blue mountain:
A traveler
goes
beyond that mountain.

Sayings of the Masters

You can't step twice into the **same** river.

Heraclitus

to be **nobody-but-yourself**—

in a world which is doing its best,

night and day,

to make you **everybody else**

—means to fight the hardest battle

which any human being can fight;

and **never stop fighting**.

e e cummings

He who **knows** he has enough is rich.

Lao Tzu

Nothing divides one
so much as thought.

R. H. Blyth

Strength doesn't come from

physical capacity.

It comes from **indomitable will**.

Mahatma Gandhi

Awaken the mind
without fixing it
anywhere.

Diamond Sutra

Discipline divorced

from wisdom

is not true discipline,

but merely the meaningless following of custom,

which is a **disguise** for ignorance.

Rabindranath Tagore

The mystery of life
is not a problem to be solved,
it is a reality to be lived.

van der Leeuwarden

The real voyage of discovery consists not in seeking new landscapes, but in having new eyes.

Marcel Proust

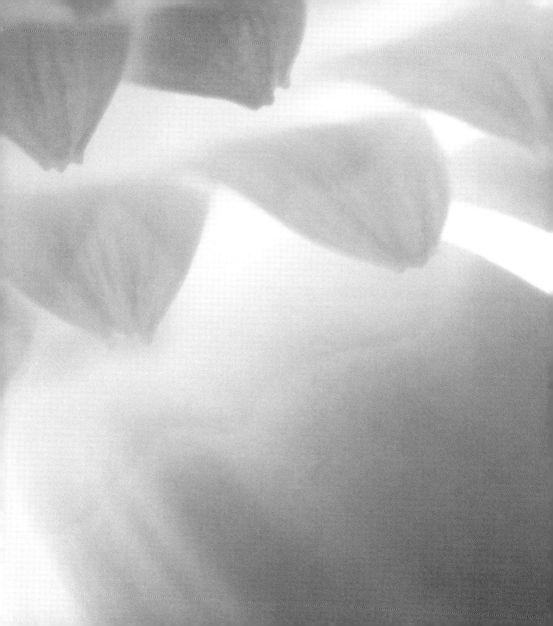

We are what we think.

All that we are arises

with our **thoughts**.

With our thoughts

we **make the world**.

Buddha

Life is either a daring adventure,
or nothing.

Helen Keller

Things don't change.

You change your **way of looking**,

that's all.

Carlos Castaneda

Enter a **tiger's cave**
and stroke its whiskers!

Sayings of the Masters

Be master of yourself

—**everywhere**:

All you do

proves true.

Sayings of the Masters

I hold to the doctrine

that with **ordinary** talent,

and **extraordinary** perseverance,

all things are attainable.

Thomas Buxton

In the beginner's mind

there are **many** possibilities,

but in the expert's mind

there are few.

Shunryu Suzuki

Our plans miscarry

because they have no **aim**.

When a man does not know

what huge **harbor** he is making for,

no wind is the right wind.

Seneca

If you wish to drown,

do not torture yourself

with **shallow** water.

Bulgarian proverb

Act without **doing**;

work without

effort.

Lao Tzu

Get rid of the self

and act from the Self!

Zen saying

You see things
and say, "why?"
but I dream things that never were
and say, "why not?"

George Bernard Shaw

Let not the fruit of action

be your **motive** to action.

Your business is with **action** alone,

not with the fruit of action.

Bhagavad Gita

Ask and it shall be **given** unto you.
Seek and ye shall find.

Luke 11:9

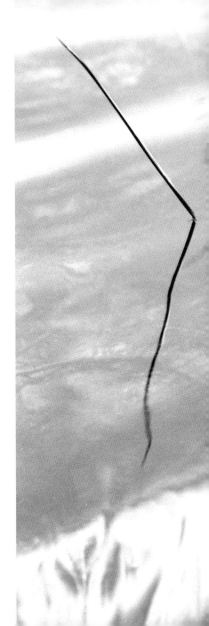

When the student

is ready,

the Master appears.

Japanese Buddhist proverb

Zen in its essence is the art of

seeing into the nature of one's being,

and it points the way

from **bondage** to freedom.

D. T. Suzuki

Never let go the reins
of the wild colt of the heart.

Japanese Buddhist proverb

It is good to have an **end** to journey toward; but it is the **journey** that matters, **in the end**.

Ursula K. Le Guin

First published in the United States in 2000 by Journey Editions, an imprint of Periplus Editions (HK) Ltd., with editorial offices at 153 Milk Street, Boston, Massachusetts 02109.

Copyright © 2000 MQ Publications Ltd

Translations of the Sayings of the Masters from *A Zen Forest* by Soiku Shigematsu published by permission of Weatherhill, Inc. Photographs of the swinging gate, ladybird, jetty, scarecrow bird box, dandelion head and broken fence are reproduced by permission of Neil Sutherland.

Editor: Alison Moss
Series designer: Plum Partnership
Designer: Yvonne Dedman

Library of Congress Catalog Card Number: 00-105192

ISBN: 1582900426

First edition
06 05 04 03 02 01 00 10 9 8 7 6 5 4 3 2 1

Printed in Italy

Distributed by

NORTH AMERICA

Tuttle Publishing
Distribution Center
Airport Industrial Park
364 Innovation Drive
North Clarendon
VT 05759-9436
Tel: (802) 773-8930
Fax: (800) 526-2778

JAPAN

Tuttle Publishing
RK Building, 2nd Floor
2-12-10 Shimo-Meguro
Meguro-Ku
Tokyo 153 0064
Tel: (03) 5437-0171
Fax: (03) 5437-0755

ASIA PACIFIC

Berkeley Books Pte Ltd
5 Little Road 08-01
Singapore 536983
Tel: (65) 280-1330
Fax: (65) 280-6290